All Aboard the Brain Train

Dr. Linda Miles
and
Dr. Amy Bunger

ISBN: Softcover   978-1-5245-8960-8
        Hardcover   978-1-5245-8961-5
        EBook   978-1-5245-8959-2

Print information available on the last page.

Rev. date: 04/04/2017

To order additional copies of this book, contact:
Xlibris
1-888-795-4274
www.Xlibris.com
Orders@Xlibris.com

Contents

DEDICATION

To the youngest, Isaac and Bella,
and to Merritt, Drew, Bobby, Samantha,
Alexandra, Genevieve, Remington,
Noelle, and Brandt,
who all grew up so fast.

Your children are not your children.
They are the sons and daughters of Life's longing for itself.
….For their souls dwell in the house of tomorrow,
Which you cannot visit, not even in your dreams.
You may strive to be like them, but seek not to make them like you,
For life goes not backward nor tarries with yesterday.

Kahlil Gibran

ACKNOWLEDGMENTS

Thanks to editors, Angela Panayotopulos and Katey Roberts, for helping shape and edit this material. Loula Fuller generously shared her expertise in early childhood education. Thanks also to Isaac Cooper, age 8, for his invaluable input.

INTRODUCTION

Babies are born with basic instincts, but they need their parents to help them make sense of the world. Based upon research involving neuroplasticity and mindfulness practices with children, we seek to provide practical and fun ways to help arm your child's brain with a calm, purpose-filled mind-set and help provide him or her with all the love, security, and courage needed to face challenges of the world. YOU have the incredible capability to affect the physical structure of a child's brain.

BUILDING STATIONS

DIRECTION AND STATIONS

*You cannot make people learn. You can only provide
the right conditions for learning to happen.*
—Vince Gowmon

STATIONS are potential destinations in the brain. Once you perceive that there are 100 billion neurons in the brain and they work across a myriad of networks of interconnections, you can begin to fathom the possibilities. You want your child to travel to positive and remarkable stations. To ensure this as much as you can, you can help build your child's brain story.

You can help route your child's brain and, therefore, their life—toward the most positive, productive *directions*. When you help build "stations" for a child, you help inspire this young person's direction, values, belief system, and life choices.

Significance, beauty, and wonder are encapsulated in a life-altering notion: when you change your story, you can change your brain.

You can help develop safe and secure stories and stations in your child's brain that can last a lifetime; you can help develop memories and thought habits that they can internalize and later refer to for comfort, strength, and information when life becomes challenging.

PURPOSE

*It is the supreme art of the teacher to awaken joy
in creative expression and knowledge.*

—Albert Einstein

Train your children to live their lives on purpose and by choice. Good parenting can help build a neural railway that offers opportunities and adventure. Parents can help structure their child's brain to develop a world full of possibilities.

Neurotransmitters send signals between neurons by initiating or inhibiting electrical activity. Think of this as the brain's chemical language. These neurotransmitters can turn certain genes on and off; by doing so, they cause long-term changes in the brain. Children need to feel that they are nurtured and safe for optimal brain development to take place.

You help shape your child's purpose because you have the ability to influence the physical and mental structure of your child's brain. You do this by helping create mental pictures of purpose-filled stations. The more trips the "train of thought" takes toward these stations, the stronger those brain connections. Neurons that wire together fire together.

By building positive and peaceful stations for babies and young children, you are providing them with an invaluable starting point for dealing with present and future challenges and frustrations. Mindfulness practices have been shown to facilitate this process.

MINDFULNESS

Our life stories are largely constructed and without mindfulness can prove destructive.

—Rasheed Ogunlaru

Mindfulness refers to the cultivation of inner peace. According to Jon Kabat-Zinn, "Mindfulness means paying attention in a particular way; on purpose, in the present moment, and non-judgementally." Parents can practice mindfulness with young children with the combined benefits of greater equanimity, increased attention, purpose-filled living, and the ability to better manage emotions.

According to the UCLA Mindful Awareness Research Center, significant research conducted during the last decade has revealed many benefits of mindfulness and its effects on our well-being and health. Among other things, mindfulness

✿ lowers blood pressure,
✿ increases our attention spans and focus,
✿ reduces depression and anxiety,
✿ reduces emotional reactivity, and
✿ expands regions in the brain that deal with decision making, empathy, and emotional flexibility.

You can make mindfulness practice a fun and consistent activity. Find a regular time for you and your child to practice, ideally daily. Eliminate as many distractions as possible. Remember that even five minutes of practice a day will add up. You can also use these practices when your child is stressed and needs to calm down; needless to say, these practices work just as well for parents. Such techniques can help you relax and reflect in order to help you become a more proactive and less reactive parent. And no one can say that you don't practice what you preach!

While we recommend some mindfulness practices for you and your child, feel free to use your imagination to create your own warm and welcoming stations for brain train destinations.

PRACTICE BUILDING STATIONS

⟹ The Breathing Buddy: Relaxing

Every station needs a *breathing buddy*. A breathing buddy is a stuffed animal of your child's choice; the child can use this stuffed friend by placing the toy lightly on his or her abdomen so that it moves up with every inhalation and down with every exhalation. This practice teaches your child that paying attention can be soothing, especially when combined with deep, meditative, refreshing breathing; the stuffed animal offers comfort and camaraderie. This is just one way to create a happy station in your child's room.

⟹ Unhooking the Boxcar: Letting Go

Imagine that something that happened during your child's day—a negative experience, in this case—is transformed into a boxcar at the back of a train that your child is directing. Have your child sit cross-legged on the floor facing you. Stretch out your arms in front of you and hold hands. Together, rock your bodies slightly to the left and to the right before centering yourselves again. Imagine together that you both just unhooked that boxcar from the back of the train and that it is released as the train moves forward. You are teaching your child to let go of negative experiences and to return to a calm, centered place in the present moment.

As the child watches the boxcar fall away, you can explain that feelings are like the train cars passing through, that come and go just like trains, and that we can detach them from the train when we don't need them anymore. Your child can begin to mindfully notice feelings as they come and go. For example, you can wave "bye" to sadness, anger, hurt, or unfulfilled wishes, and then you can watch those **boxcar emotions** move away—or as you, on the train, move away from those feelings.

So alternatively, you could have your child imagine that they can take negative events that happened during the day and load them onto the train to move away. Ask them what events from that day they might want to load into the boxcars on the train. You can say "Bye, bad time." You are training the useful technique of mindfulness that involves simply watching without judgement.

It is up to you whether it is the train or the boxcar that is moving away. What is important is the concept of release and of moving on. In this way you help the child acknowledge negative events without holding on to them. You can also ask, what did you learn from what happened after sending the car away . . .

✐ Boxcar Emotions and Station Sanctuaries

Children love repetition; fortunately, practice makes permanent in the brain. Make an ongoing game to visit the stations and tape faces on boxcars called Mad, Sad, and Glad. You are helping the child begin to understand emotions by labels. You are also helping emphasize the concept that feelings come and go. By building a calming station in his or her room, and filling it with friends like the stuffed animals that stay at the station, you are teaching the child how to self-soothe, showing the child that they can return to a safe place and not be carried off by emotions.

Ask children to describe what their perfect station would be like. Who would be there? A puppy? A kitten? Parents? Friends? Tell them that they should have a warm and fun place to which they can always return to when they're afraid or upset. For adults, this is called a freeze-frame technique where you imagine that your mind can unearth, when needed, a snapshot—or freeze-frame—of a place or time when you felt calm, safe, loved, and nurtured.

To create a tangible station that will become a soothing sanctuary, start by creating a *wonder book* with your child. Cut out and paste within the book some pictures that he or she has chosen, pictures that personally represent joy and meaning. These can be arranged in a collage. In this way, the child begins to pay attention to what is soothing and how positive past experiences are triggered in the present moment. Keep the wonder book of happy pictures nearby in the child's room so that he or she can refer to it whenever needed.

> Do not educate your children to be rich. Educate them to be happy, so that when they grow up they know the value of things, not the price.
> —Anonymous

LAY TRACKS

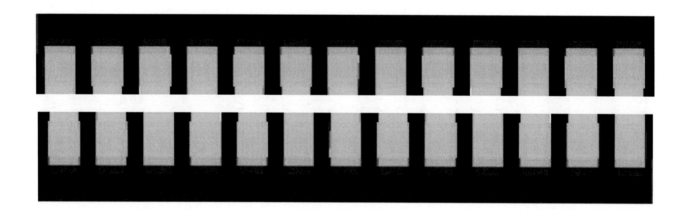

A FOUNDATION OF LOVE

Every day, in a 100 small ways, our children ask: "Do you hear me? Do you see me? Do I matter?" Their behavior often reflects our response.

—L. R. Knost

Your child's feelings and choices are based on what little of the world they actually understand and can relate to with their blossoming brains.

TELL YOUR CHILD "I'M SO GLAD YOU WERE BORN!" THIS MAKES THEM FEEL IMPORTANT TO YOU AND THE FAMILY AND HELPS THEM FEEL SAFE AND LOVED. FEELING POSITIVE REDUCES ANXIETY, ENABLING CHILDREN TO LEARN AND EXPLORE MORE FEARLESSLY AND EFFECTIVELY.

Lean down so your child hugs your heart instead of your knees! Children require affection and connection to grow healthy bodies and brains. Remember that the brain is a social organism; the security of a child's relationship with you is necessary to uncover directions that they want to pursue and to stimulate their imagination. Children love the game where you hold them up or when you kneel to their level because they get to feel big and powerful.

A ROADMAP TO THE DREAM

If children feel safe, they can take risks, ask questions, make mistakes, learn to trust, share their feelings, and grow.
—Alfie Kohn

Since baby brains are works in progress, help train your child's brain to lay tracks in the direction of their dreams. Remember, your child understands the world in terms of "all or nothing," black and white. They need to be exposed to as many purposeful possibilities and options as possible. Just as there are endless ways and places to connect train tracks, the child should see that there are just as many ways to reach a destination, especially since some ways will be blocked or ridden with danger.

The practice of positive repetition builds strong tracks that lead toward a more meaningful life. Help your child's brain get into **GEAR** by preaching and practicing

- ✿ Growth
- ✿ Empathy
- ✿ Acceptance
- ✿ Responsibility

Steer your child toward making good life choices using *affirmations* and imagery. Often repeat positive ideas and thoughts, such as

✿ "You can do it, and I will help."
✿ "You did that really well, thank you."
✿ "It's okay to take your time."
✿ "I love you."
✿ "It's okay to ask for help."
✿ "You're a good friend."
✿ "When you make mistakes, try again."

You must be your children's greatest support system and their most avid cheerleader. Joseph Campbell has said, "Follow your bliss." This famous professor of mythology learned this from his mother. She encouraged his childhood fascination with Native Americans by taking him to museums and encouraging him to collect arrowheads. This attuned mother helped her son grow his interest and imagination. The destinations that parents help set can motivate children for a lifetime.

THE ROAD TO HAPPINESS

*Let the child be the scriptwriter, the director,
and the actor in his own play.*

—Magda Gerber

Lie on the floor and pretend to be train tracks. Ask your child what he or she wants to visit today. Let your child be your teacher who shows you the *happy place* on your body. You can help by pointing to your knees or elbows and asking, "Is the happy place here?" Have your child describe the smells, sounds, and sights of the imaginary happy place.

Happiness is contagious. A smile infuses chemicals into the body that shift and lift moods. Laughter is prosperity even during the greatest hardship. Looking for opportunities to be silly and light-hearted expands the imagination and vision. Developing this sort of attitude will help your child better deal with life's inevitable derailments down the road.

PRACTICE: LAY TRACKS

✈ Train Sounds: Focus

Find an application on your computer or cell phone that features the sound of a train whistle as the train is receding. Help your child pay close attention until he or she cannot hear the sound anymore. Ask your child to tell you when the sound ends. You are training the brain to pay attention and focus on what is happening in the present moment.

✈ Mental Trains: Thoughts

Run your finger across the top of your child's head and playfully ask your child to imagine a train that runs inside his or her head. Ask the child to watch as a train moves and leaves, eventually disappearing in a mental cloud. Just like this train, explain that thoughts also move around in this manner, coming and going. You can say "Bye-bye, thought" as he or she thinks of something. Ask "Do you have a new thought now?" Then wave goodbye to that thought to make room for another new one. Make it a game to watch thoughts come and go, as you playfully ask "Are you having one now?"

✈ Train Sounds: Self-Affirmation

Have your child repeat over and over, in harmony as with the clicking of a train chugging across the tracks, "I like myself the way I am". Talk about how we all make mistakes and sometimes are headed in the wrong direction, but it is much easier to find ourselves and turn ourselves around if we have self-compassion. We want the train to travel in directions that are beneficial for us *and* others.

✈ Naming Boxcars: Positive Emotions

Ask your child to have a boxcar on the train called Happy Times; this is where he or she can load the positive experiences. Although these experiences may come and go, the child can bring back the boxcar as often as he or she desires, simply by wishing it back or recalling the memory. Together, you can draw or take pictures of happy times, then fold them up or place them in a box that represents the Happiness boxcar.

Just so, you can develop a boxcar named Grateful and let your child put inside pictures or drawings of things for which he or she is grateful. This helps your child learn to practice appreciation, especially for everyday things which most people take for granted. Acknowledge all the good things that happen to you. Come back to these to practice gratitude and remember all the things for which you can give thanks for together.

Navigating Tracks: Finding Your Way and Managing Conflict

Explain to your child that the fuel for the train is joy and laughter every day. Children—as well as adults—need to find things to celebrate, things that bring them joy, so that their tank is never empty. Together, recall fun experiences from the day and help your child see how such experiences provide positive energy. Ask what fuel you can put in today to help the train move forward.

MARCHING DOWN THE TRACKS TOGETHER

March together like the train clicking down the tracks and sing "I am a happy me" so that the two of you repeat this over and over: "I am happy! I am a happy me!" You can also use the tracks as an example of how to realign yourself and literally "get back on track" when your child has made a mistake or has had a bad day. Show your child how to switch between tracks by sharing your own mistakes using humor and accountability, displaying a willingness to apologize.

RAILWAY REPAIR

Understanding train tracks can also enable your child to "fix" them when necessary instead of rerouting. Bang two toy trains against each other and explain to your child that sometimes people bang into each other like two trains and that it's important to stop and fix the connection so that the train runs smoothly again. Help your child identify train wrecks that happen during the day and talk about ways to fix them. Get him or her involved; ask "How can we fix this train wreck?"

A man never stands as tall as when he kneels to help a child.
—Knights of Pythagoras

REROUTE-OVER-UNDER-AROUND-THROUGH

OVERCOMING OBSTACLES

Please excuse the mess, children are making memories.

—Anonymous

Parents can help their children find ways to reroute by getting over, under, around, or through their obstacles, while using more of the brain's potential. Assure your child that having feelings is a natural experience that makes us all human, but draw the line at destructive behavior. Acting on feelings that disrespect others is not okay. Help your child learn to think about what he feels and use another strategy when he or she is handling the feelings destructively.

One great way to do this is by brainstorming specific actions (or reactions) ahead of time. For example, you can help children name their feelings—i.e., sad, glad, or mad—and then move toward positive decision solutions.

When children realize that there is trouble ahead, they need your help to create positive solutions. They need your guidance to "switch tracks" and realign themselves with constructive emotions and goals. You can easily show your child how to switch tracks by sharing your mistakes and establishing empathy and camaraderie, by using humor to lighten a situation and show more perspectives, and by displaying a willingness to apologize and showing how to be accountable and thoughtful as you lead by example.

IN CASE OF TRAIN WRECKS

I believe that to teach them effectively, you must touch their hearts long before you begin to teach their minds.

—Vicki Savini

FAMILY TRAIN WRECKS

When a *train wreck* occurs—and it is as inevitable as our human nature is—it is important to repair your connection with your child to maintain his or her sense of safety. A key element is to be proactive, instead of reactive when the train wrecks. Make sure your child is running on a "full tank" of love and positivity. You can refuel your child's "engine" with love, laughter, and positive reaffirmations every day. A train can't run on an empty tank or with limited fuel, and neither can a healthy human being.

BEST BAD DAYS

Show your child how to have a "best bad day." Help your child lay new tracks through adversity by facing derailment with spirit. Encourage your child to ask for information to make good decisions; this will create more routes and breakthroughs. Teach your child to take responsibility for his or her behavior instead of blaming others; set an example by doing this yourself. Examine situations and discuss their causes, accept responsibility and apologize when appropriate, and actively seek solutions instead of marinating in misery. If there is nothing that can be done, then discuss what lessons can be learned. Sometimes acceptance is the best way through a challenging situation.

Showing is always more powerful than telling.

PACE THE TRAIN

Everybody is a genius. But if you judge a fish by its ability to climb a tree, it will live its whole life believing that it is stupid.
—Albert Einstein

Allow children to enjoy their childhood, and ensure that you make time to cherish these fleeting years. If children grow up too soon, they miss the magic of imagination, and this void fills with the burdening notion that they must solve the family problems. It is important that children don't feel the weight of your own problems, so handle them yourself.

This is not to say that children should be locked away in a self-centered cocoon of obliviousness. They are aware of the existence of problems and the need to define and resolve them. And of course, life will always set up an obstacle course—that is the adventure of the journey after all. Transmit a problem-solving attitude to your child.

When children do not get the response they want, teach them to look first at options to change their own behavior instead of trying to change others.

PRACTICE REROUTE- OVER-UNDER- AROUND-THROUGH

Following Tracks: Motion Causing Emotion

A good mindfulness strategy for children and parents is to allow your attention to drop down to your feet so that you just notice sensations—you'll find that you breathe more deeply and more calmly, as your mind focuses on a specific task and you attune yourself with the sensations happening to you.

Stand beside your child and tell them that you're both going to start paying attention to your feet. Together, you're going to imagine that there are tracks on the floor beneath your feet; begin to shuffle your feet to mimic the wheels of a train. You can make noises like "Choo-Choo!" as your feet move shuffle forward. Ask your child what it feels like to move his or her feet along the imaginary (or drawn) tracks. Help the child focus on the sensations in his or her feet as you both move along.

The magic of this activity isn't just that you and your child are practicing mindfulness by focusing on the sensations of walking the tracks. You are also physically moving forward, and you can use this as a metaphor or a mental analogy to show how you are being proactive and taking control of your direction and destiny. You can also imagine (or create) obstacles ahead of your child (a small wall made of pillows, for example) as you walk along the tracks together; discuss how you'd overcome each obstacle (going through, around, over, or under it) in order to keep moving forward. Then do it. Encourage and celebrate the overcoming of each hurdle.

Moving Boxcars: Practice Compassion

Remember those boxcars you created and labeled? Find the one called Happy. Together, imagine that you and your child can send this Happy boxcar to visit other people who are having a sad day. Have your child take the initiative by asking him or her who looked or acted today in a way that seemed sad; ask "Who do you think needs the boxcar?" This encourages your child to reflect on other people's emotions and take constructive steps toward helping them.

It's even better if you act upon the thought. How many times has a child made your day by offering you a smile, a flower, a drawing, a rock, or anything considered precious to them? If a child literally walks up to someone and gives them a "Happiness Boxcar" and explains that it brings things meant to make the other person happy—it may make that person's day. Such activities enable you and your child to practice compassion.

I've learned that people will forget what you said, people will forget what you did, but people will never forget how you made them feel.
—Maya Angelou

MOMMY/DADDY AS ENGINEER

DEVELOPING NEW PATTERNS

Teach children what to think and you limit them to your ideas.
Teach children how to think and their ideas are unlimited.

—Sandra Parks

As the engineer and conductor of the train, a parent is enabled to create and learn new patterns along with his or her child. As a parent, your own life experiences, your childhood and adulthood, and all the lessons you've learned along the way have armed you with the expertise you need as "engineer" on your child's train tracks. Your family values and aspirations help provide a blueprint for railroad routes so that, together with your child, you can explore beautiful and creative vistas.

It is perfectly human and natural to make mistakes, but repeating mistakes is a mindless habit. People who see the same mistakes or patterns time and time again need to lay new tracks. Remember that the brain retains its neuroplasticity throughout life; it is flexible with the incredible capability of being rewired. You can free yourself and your child from destructive derailments that may have been even carried through generations in your family. Lay new tracks made with positivity. Change your story and change your brain.

LEAD BY EXAMPLE

Kids don't remember what you try to teach them. They remember what you are.

—Jim Henson

Show your child how to celebrate life. Children learn best from example: they analyze *who we are*, as parents, and *what we do*—and not as much *what we say*. If you preach one thing and practice another, the thing that you practice carries more weight than the thing that you preach.

SHARING

As a parent, sharing stories about your own life is a wonderful avenue and opportunity to share and instill values. Plus, you get the bonus of lots of snuggle time. Secure and loving relationships are more possible when the parents make sense of their own individual lives and roles. When you share your stories, it also helps your child become more conscious and understanding of you, your world, and your choices.

LIVING YOUR WAY TO THE ANSWER

When your child poses questions or challenges that you don't have answers for, it is okay to accept and share that you are learning too. Sometimes you have to find your way to answers by undergoing new experiences. You may need to "live your way to the answer." It is very important for your child to witness your life because you are modeling problem solving.

FOLLOWING THE LEADER

*It's not our job to toughen our children up to face a cruel
and heartless world. It's our job to raise children who will
make the world a little less cruel and heartless.*

—L. R. Knost

Your children need to see you as a person—not just as a parent. If you didn't learn to play as a child, take how-to-play lessons from your own child; it isn't coincidental that, as the saying goes, raising children provides you with a "second childhood" in many ways. Playing infuses our brains with positive chemicals that can drastically improve both mental and physical health.

You need to protect your family—yourself and especially your children—by surrounding yourself with a network of positive role models. This includes people who show how to celebrate life. Find healthy people who can model joy, especially during hard times. Both you and your child can learn from these models—your child, especially, needs concrete examples to learn from. Therefore, use the same care in choosing *your* friends as you would to help your child choose theirs. Remember that we each have a "family of origin" and a "family of choice." If your family of origin has been disappointing, you can adopt the family of choice.

Work backward when raising your children. Work with the end in mind. Think of the adult you want your children to grow to be.

PRACTICE MOMMY/ DADDY AS ENGINEER

⚐ Leading by Example: Appreciation

Be your child's role model in teaching (by showing) appreciation. Show them that the little things are actually the big things in life—especially the everyday things which most people take for granted. You can practice what you preach by taking the initiative and doing something special together for someone else in your lives. Giving to others provides the best grade of "happiness fuel" for you and your child's engines. Even the smallest actions, when done with an open heart, are extremely meaningful:

- ⚙ Surprise a teacher with lunch
- ⚙ Give greeting cards and stamps to an elderly neighbor
- ⚙ Bake and take a plate of cookies to someone "just because"

⚐ Leading by Example: Celebration

Celebrate things considered ordinary, everyday, or things which are typically unappreciated:

- ⚙ The first day of autumn
- ⚙ Christmas in July
- ⚙ A puppy
- ⚙ A piece of delicious ripe fruit
- ⚙ A sunny day
- ⚙ A fun day at the park
- ⚙ A picture your child has drawn

⚐ Leading by Example: Daily Rituals and Affirmations

Develop *rituals* with your child:

- ⚙ Share gratitude at dinner; you can each keep a *gratitude journal* (i.e., with the top three things you're thankful for that day) and share your thoughts when you gather at the table.
- ⚙ Read before bed.
- ⚙ Take a walk to start or end the day together.
- ⚙ Play catch or Frisbee with your child and pets.
- ⚙ Suggest a tea party.
- ⚙ Dance a happy dance together.

☀ Sing a song—or write one.
☀ Do a craft together.

Train your brain as well as your child's brain to commit to *positive affirmations*. Remember that decisions made as a child may dominate a person's adult life. Model and talk about how you find the best creative solutions for problems. Your child will follow your example.

☀ "I'm a happy me."
☀ "I love myself."
☀ "I'm a good dancer."
☀ "I'm a good friend."
☀ "I have a nice smile."
☀ "I can be brave even when I am afraid."

Additional Practices for Parents

Visit www.Drlindamiles.com to discover many more practices and games that will help parents relax, enjoy, and make the most of their time as they are bonding and learning with their children.

To be in your children's memories tomorrow,
you have to be in their lives today.

—Anonymous

Conclusion

True to the balance of nature and nurture, the environment's influence on your little human being is inevitable. Here's what you *do* have control over: your own scope of influence. That's the strength, longevity, and depth of your nurturing love.

You'll discover that influencing someone with nurturing love will be the one of the most fulfilling and meaningful things you'll ever accomplish in your lifetime. With your compassion, positivity, patience, dedication, and knowledge, you can nurture your child's soul and guide them toward a world full of possibility and a happy adulthood..

Wishing you a lifetime of learning, love, and laughter!

Linda and Amy

Made in the USA
San Bernardino, CA
27 April 2018